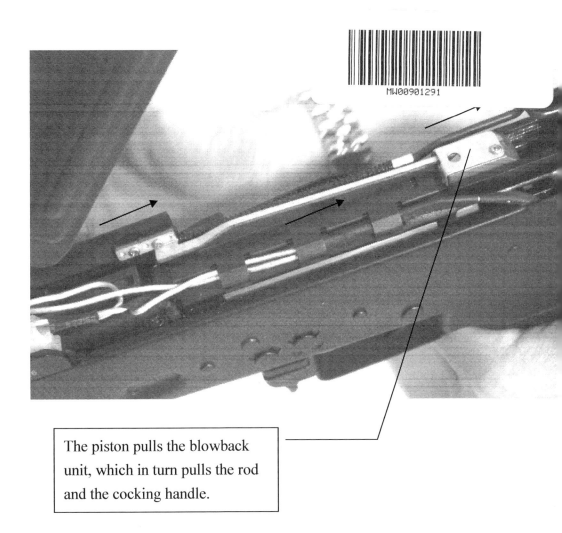

The piston pulls the blowback unit, which in turn pulls the rod and the cocking handle.

When the piston moves backward, it pulls the blowback u together. The mechanism is simple and effective. Note the that pulls the cocking handle backward. Also note the rang movement – the travel distance is not that long.

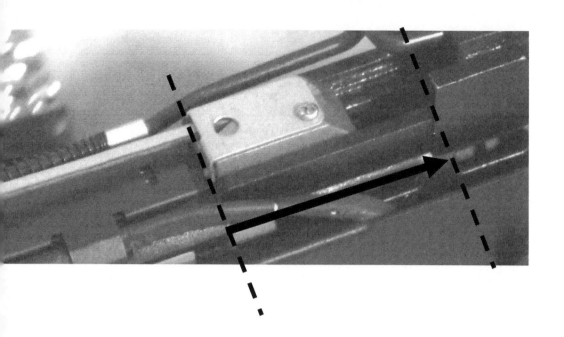

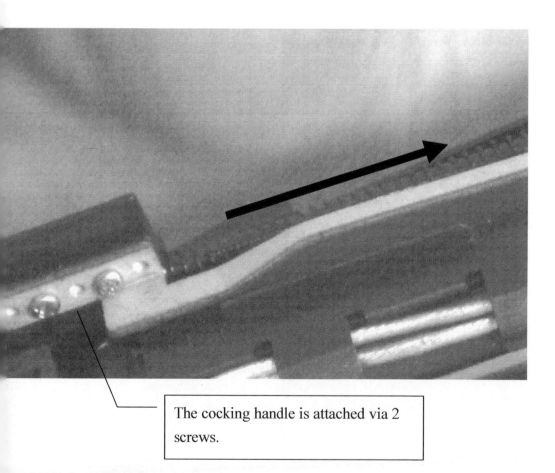

The cocking handle is attached via 2 screws.

# D60

## TRANSFORMATION THROUGH
## DISCIPLESHIP

*A sixty-day ascent from where you are to where you could not have imagined!*

Written by **Stephen Meeks** | Edited by **Hope Cooper**
Designed by **Brooklyn Sims**

ISBN-10:149431620X

Published by GSMi Press

5279 Highway 297

Pioneer, TN 37847

# ACKNOWLEDGMENTS

Leadership expert John C. Maxwell wrote, "Everyone is part of a team." Books are the result of teamwork. My D60 team and I have done our best to present, in clear and practical form, a blueprint for your spiritual success, and I want to acknowledge each of them.

Hope Cooper carried her first child as she worked through the initial editing of D60. I appreciate not only her investment of time, but also her encouraging words for "Mr. Steve". Hope, your name fits you perfectly. Thanks for the cheers!

Mark Miller, Hope's dad, whom we referred to in our emails as "Dear ole Dad", meticulously weeded through the grammatical stuff. I so much appreciate detail-people—not being one myself. May their tribe increase! Thank you, Mark, for your help. By the way, you have a really handsome grandson. Congratulations!

Brooklyn Sims came along at the perfect time. A gifted artist and delightful lady, Brooklyn handled all the graphic design elements of D60. Please, see more of her work at www.simsadventures.com. I cannot express how much I appreciate, not only her hours invested in this project, but her joyful eagerness to help. She exemplifies the heart of a disciple of Jesus. Thank you, Brooklyn!

Lastly, I want to acknowledge my bride, Donna. After a day of home school, hosting guests, and handling everyone else's crises, you made the final check of this material. Midnight had long past when I peeked in on you. Exhausted, I saw your eyes close, your head gently nod, and then you forcing yourself back to consciousness, pen in hand, to go at it again. Thank you for helping me, as you do so many. What a friend. What a gift. What a lady. You'll always be the first I pick for my team!

# WHY D60?

The source of true spiritual strength is where it has always been--in the Savior. It is the actual presence of the person of Jesus in our lives that recreates us. It is He who transforms from the inside out, but less and less we see it happening.

Millennials, obsessed over the threat of global-warming, ignore their personal-warming toward the habits, attitudes, and behaviors destroying their own lives. Moral purity and political correctness are blurred; the virtue of agape love is replaced with tolerance, and social justice has become the substitute for the Savior's blood! There are powerful spiritual forces at work, and we need strong leadership in the face of them, but where are those leaders?

Christian men--clergy and laity alike-- are falling weak-kneed and helpless before the idol of pornography, and their faith seems powerless to help them. Christians in their twenties and thirties are often either unapologetically apathetic or deeply angry at the Church—or God Himself. They ironically embrace the values of Jesus, such as kindness, humility, goodness, and compassion, but view faith in Him as embarrassing, misguided, or unnecessary. Things are upside down.

What is your opinion? Would you describe most Christians today as spiritually strong or spiritually flabby? Too many are spiritually unfit. It is time for strengthening, but preacher pep-talks, moving music, and inspirational devotionals are not doing the job, and they won't do it because transformational power does not reside in them. We need the Savior's presence in our lives, and we need it soon! This is why D60 is written.

D60 is a plan that enables God to change people by putting them in His presence. Over eight weeks of spiritual discipleship there is deep and decisive transformation. What about you? Are you ready for the Savior's spiritual strengthening? Would you allow Him to transform your life? The world and the church are in great need of the spiritually strong. Please, lead us.

# Table of Contents

# FRONT WORDS

●●●●●●●●●●●●●●●●●●●●●●●●●●●●●●●●●●●●●●●●●●●●●●

## A WORD OF ENCOURAGEMENT
## to the "Spiritually Flabby"

The 1970's movie "Rocky" inspires me. It isn't the bloody pounding of his opponents, nor his muscular physique, nor the lovely Adrian that stir me. What moves me is Rocky's heart.

As the movie begins, however, Rocky isn't very motivating. In fact, Rocky isn't rocky at all; he's more like dough. The Italian Stallion is a talent with potential but still a nobody. His grizzled mentor and coach, Mickey, even jabs at the Stallion's lackadaisical life when, with graveled voice he exasperatedly spits, "You're a nobody. You're a bum because ya lack heart, kid. Ya lack the heart!" The young fighter, for all his talent, did lack heart, but that would change dramatically. Rocky's defining quality would surface, and he'd prove that he had the heart of a true champion.

The transformation from loser to champ began one pre-dawn hour with the out-of-shape, sleepy-eyed has-been dragging himself from a warm bed into a frosty living room. Leaning on the refrigerator for balance, he opens its door. Wincing at the fridge's

light, he cracks almost a dozen eggs into a glass. The audience then cringes in disbelief as he quaffs the whole dozen eggs. Whoa! The a.m. eggs portend, "Okay. He's for real." Alone in the pre-dawn darkness, he jabs the cold damp air a couple of times, cranks his head from side to side as if limbering up, and then shuffles into a half-hearted jog. Day by day training intensifies until one morning the music changes, the tempo picks up, trumpets blare in the background, neighbors cheer him through the streets, and his jog turns into a sprint. Charging up the steps of the Philadelphia Museum of Art, he lifts his arms in victory as the sun breaks over the horizon. Our emotions rise too. The transformation is complete-- now we're talkin' ROCKY, baby!

Today many Christians are more like the out-of-shape, half-hearted "Stallion" than the chiseled Rocky Balboa. They gorge themselves on spiritual fast food: trendy efforts, large religious events, and emotive music— that supports an under-exercised faith. Lacking a strenuous depth of conviction and a personal appetite for holiness, they are spiritually flabby. I think that if Mickey were coaching them he'd be growling, "Bums! Ya lack the heart." The sad truth is he'd be right. Transformation requires more than great songs and good sermons prepared by others; transformation results from personal investment.

Remember the guy who only ate at McDonald's for weeks? His good health actually fell from vibrancy toward illness. There is a corollary (I almost wrote coronary) spiritually: unless we consume spiritually nourishing food and practice spiritual exercise, we will weaken and die spiritually. Christians have been misled into believing *that our souls consume* is as important as *what our souls consume*. It isn't true. *What* we consume makes all the difference. A healthy, strong relationship with God depends on what we take into our minds and how we use it. Many will consume, but not all will strengthen.

Since the documentary on the McDonald's guy, has the fast-food industry grown or shrunk? Despite a documented warning, most Americans continue to eat foods that appear to diminish their health. Many cheered for the underdog-come-champ in Stallone's film, but how many went for a jog the next morning, let alone slugged a glass of raw eggs? As important as inspiration can be, it doesn't substitute for application. The attractive promises of <u>D60</u> will not move everyone off their spiritual couches. As surely as push-ups build biceps, the practices outlined in this book will strengthen you spiritually. Those who complete the exercises in <u>D60</u> will be changed. Jesus said, "Few will find it," (Matthew 7:14). Be one of the few. Make up your mind to complete every exercise to the best of your ability. As the first sign of your commitment to spiritual transformation, initial and date this pledge--

*I am committed to spiritual transformation:* _____ Date: _____.

If you signed, you're already among those most likely to exchange their spiritual junk food for growth in Christ. There is a reason you've committed to begin this work of transformation. It's why you'll keep fighting even when you are too busy, feeling tired, or not getting results. You'll do it because you have the heart of THE Champion. Listen! Hear them? You aren't on your own. There's a heavenly stadium cheering for YOU! From this day forward never look back, listen up. Let's go on a sixty-day run.

*"Therefore, since we are surrounded by such a great cloud of witnesses, let us throw off every thing that hinders and the sin that so easily entangles, and let us run with perseverance the race marked out for us."* **--Hebrews 12:1**

*"Run in such a way as to win the prize."* **--1 Corinthians 9:24**

●●●●●●●●●●●●●●●●●●●●●●●●●●●●●●●●●●●●●●●●●●●●●●●●●●●●●

# A WORD OF INSTRUCTION
## on Spiritual Transformation

Spiritual transformation is a mystery to many, but here's how it works:

Begin with what you know about building physical muscle to understand spiritual transformation. Stamina and physical strengthening are the results of diet control and consistent exercise over time. Spiritual strength involves the practice of regular exercises and proper spiritual feeding.  Muscle isn't built overnight and neither is a strong spirituality.

There are three necessary elements to spiritual transformation:

1. One must start.
2. One must practice regularly.
3. One must continue.

Owning workout DVDs doesn't build muscles; exercise builds muscle.  Merely owning a Bible will not produce spiritual fitness.  In Matthew 7:24, Jesus said anyone who puts His words *into practice* will be strong-- like a house on a rock foundation.  Over the next sixty days, if you follow the <u>D60</u> workout plan, the Spirit of God will strengthen within you, and you will grow spiritual muscle.

<u>D60</u> is strong on the development of daily HABITS.  The keyword is HABITS.  Got that?  It's ALL about HABITS.  You will succeed or fail based upon how well you establish HABITS that produce spiritual strength.  God is consistent.  Scripture refers to Him as faithful, unchanging, the same yesterday, today, and forever. Even creation reflects this quality as the sun, moon, and stars consistently perform their duties. Consistency is a spiritual trait. The consistent (HABITual) practice of the spiritual disciplines cannot be overstressed. Being HABITual, consistent, faithful in the DAILY practice of the <u>D60</u> plan is key.  Again, a keyword in <u>D60</u> is  HABITS.

Practicing different habits is necessary to any improvement or change.  Have you run a 10k race, lost weight, or gotten a tan?  What changed you from non-runner to racer, from overweight to thin, from pale to richly tan?  You had to make changes in your routines and follow new habits.

Personally, I'm not a tan-man. My own legs are beyond pale—they are blindingly translucent.  I'm not a runner either. In fact, the last time I entered a race was the 100-yard dash in middle school gym class.  (I finished near the front, and figured I'd get out while on top.)  It is an understatement to admit that I am no expert on running or tanning; however, it's no secret that tanned people do not get their tans by sitting at home telling themselves,

"Okay, Body, here we go, 'Tan. Tan! Tan baby; tan for me!'" Sincere desire for a tan will not darken an inch of flesh. Likewise, no one loses weight by commanding his or her excess, "Go away fat. Go. Go. Go!!!" It obviously takes more than a <u>Runners' World</u> subscription to become a marathoner. Yet, believe it or not, these are common approaches to spiritual growth!

I will illustrate. Joe Believer decides to control his speech and makes a sincere commitment before God never to cuss again. He buys the stop-cussing best seller <u>1001 Ways to Get a Grip on Your Tongue</u>, and promises to God and himself, "I'm not going to cuss again. I won't. I won't. I won't cuss. Go away cussing. Go. Go. Go!!" Mission accomplished, he speaks the language of angels until along comes a hammer and smashes ol' Joe's thumb. Before there is time to think, he forgets his commitment and loses control. Angels cover their ears, and, holding his throbbing finger, Joe has failed. Poor Joe. What now? Like most of us, he again pledges-- more fervently than ever—not to cuss again. We admire him, but we know how it will go, don't we? Poor Joe. Poor us.

We can all relate to Joe and his dilemma. Christians fail to defeat many types of sin. The reason is that our approach to overcoming sin is flawed. Sheer willpower cannot defeat what only Jesus can conquer. Anyone using Joe's ineffective approach will fail again and again. It's a discouraging cycle, but there is an answer. Keep reading.

For ten years I lived in the region of Kenya, East Africa where many of the world's top class runners live. At elevations of 7000'-10,000' the Kalenjin people are lean and lithe. I've watched in amazement as they train. In long, effortless strides they float almost silently across the hills and valleys of their mountainous homeland. Yet, not even these elite athletes sprint a marathon their first day out. All long distance runners begin with a strategy of new habits and consistent, patient practice.

If I attempt to sprint a hard 10k my first day, I'll either injure myself or just burn out and quit. Serious athletes develop and improve themselves over a period of time. Spiritual strengthening also requires strategy and practice. THE KEY to spiritual fitness boils down to the practice of DAILY

HABITS. Spiritual growth cannot be achieved by will power or self-talk; it comes only through the disciplined use of our eyes, ears, hands, feet, and mind. Romans 6:13-14 says, "Do not offer the parts of your body to sin, as instruments of wickedness, but rather offer yourselves to God, as those who have been brought from death to life; and offer the parts of your body to him as instruments of righteousness."

> The development of **consistency** in the practice of spiritual disciplines is THE KEY to becoming spiritually fit.

# A WORD OF EXPLANATION
## What is the <u>D60</u> Difference?

<u>D60</u> is a spiritual workout plan. The goal of these routines is spiritual fitness -- a healthy relationship with God. Run a mile every day, add a half mile per week, and in a few months you'll be sprinting a 10k. Faithfully practice the exercises in <u>D60</u> and your relationship with God will strengthen and deepen.

Certainly, the exercises in <u>D60</u> aren't the only spiritual exercises. You may have tried some of the exercises before, and remained spiritually weak, but there is a distinct difference with <u>D60</u>. The difference in <u>D60</u> is HOW the disciplines are applied. <u>D60</u> advocates an approach that is long-term in its view but daily in its application. Spiritual disciplines are not shots of testosterone. They aren't pills to pop for a quick-fix or a feel-good. They are food and exercise intended to transform the inner man rather than modify behavior. <u>D60</u> coaches you through the process of developing life-long HABITS. Consistent practice of these habits places you in the presence of God where HE will transform you like the sun darkens pale skin; like exercise turns flab into lean muscle.

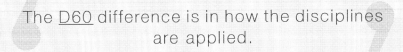

> The D60 difference is in how the disciplines are applied.

# A WORD OF TEACHING
## On the notion of bearing fruit

Our many failed efforts at overcoming sin in our lives leave us weary and clutching our sides like Rocky on his first jog up those stairs. A lasting victory over sin appears an insurmountable summit to some. Neither confessing to an entire church, "I regret my mistakes, and commit to do better", nor privately recommitting, "I will not be angry again. I will not. I promise I will not. I will not!" have proven effective before. Why keep trying? "Try, try, again," is not welcome news. Sincere intentions are no match for the obstacle of the fleshly nature. We do not do better, because we cannot do better. Yet, there is hope of winning this battle.

Re-read John 15: 1-8. I say, RE-read it, because you've probably read it many times, but it may have become so familiar that you've missed its teaching entirely.

> *I am the true vine, and my Father is the gardener. He cuts off every branch in me that bears no fruit, while every branch that does bear fruit he prunes so that it will be even more fruitful. You are already clean because of the word I have spoken to you. Remain in me, and I will remain in you. No branch can bear fruit by itself; it must remain in the vine. Neither can you bear fruit unless you remain in me. I am the vine; you are the branches. If a man remains in me and I in him, he will bear much fruit; apart from me you can do nothing. If anyone does not remain in me, he is like a branch that is thrown away and withers; such branches are picked up, thrown into the fire and burned. If you remain in me and my words remain in you, ask whatever you wish, and it will be given*

*you. This is to my Father's glory, that you bear much fruit, showing yourselves to be my disciples.*

What did Jesus tell his disciples to do? You say, "That's easy. He told them to bear fruit." Read it again. Jesus did NOT tell them to bear fruit!!! The LORD informed his disciples that the very opposite was the only thing of which they were capable, "No branch can bear fruit by itself."

Branches cannot bear fruit. A branch on its own dies. It can't even sustain itself. Fruit is not possible for a branch. Neither is peace, patience, self-control, goodness, or faithfulness possible for us.

Look again at the passage and see that what Jesus instructed his disciples to do was, "abide in me" or "remain in me." This resulted in MUCH fruit! Do you want to be spiritually alive, productive, and spiritually healthy? Connect to the Vine.

## The battle ground is the mind.

The one thing Jesus expected his disciples to do was "...remain in Him." They are told to "abide in the vine." Paul, in Galatians 5:16, expresses this too, "So I say, live by the Spirit, and you WILL NOT gratify the desires of the sinful nature." In Romans 8:12, Paul repeats himself saying, "...Brothers we have an obligation—but it is not to the sinful nature, to live according to it," and he explains, "...by the Spirit you put to death the misdeeds of the body..." Living by the Spirit, abiding in the vine, and remaining in Him signal the way for Joe Believer to stop his cussing, Sally Saint to have victory over her resentment, and Mike Martyr to overcome his pornography addiction!

The obvious question is, how are you to "abide in the vine"? Exactly what does "living by the Spirit" look like, and what does Jesus mean by "remain in me"? Scripture answers in Romans 8:5, "Those who live according to the sinful nature have their **minds** set on what that nature desires; but those who live in accordance with the Spirit have their **minds** set on what that nature desires….the **mind** controlled by the Spirit is life and peace." Your thoughts control your actions. The battlefield is the mind. It is here that the sinful nature is defeated.

The war for your soul is fought, won, or lost in the arena of the mind-- in the world of our thoughts. Paul tells the disciples in Colossae, "Set your **minds** on things above where Christ is seated…" (Colossians 3:1-2). This harmonizes with Romans 8:6, "The **mind** controlled by the Spirit is life and peace", and "Those controlled by the Spirit have their **minds** set on what the Spirit desires."

Putting your mind on Christ affords the Spirit an opportunity to work in you and change you. Romans 12: 2 says, "Do not conform any longer to the pattern of this world, but be transformed *by the renewing of your mind*." 2 Corinthians 3:18 agrees, "We who with unveiled faces all reflect the LORD's glory are being transformed into His likeness with ever increasing glory, which comes from the LORD, who is the Spirit." Transformation is God's work. Our job is to place our thoughts in His presence and on what concerns Him. This is how you connect to The Vine. This is living under the control of the Spirit. This is what Jesus meant when He assured His followers they'd be fruitful if they remained in Him.

> Spiritual fitness is a healthy relationship with God.

The following chapters are filled with exercises designed to help you abide in Christ. Each chapter's exercise builds on the previous one, increasing both your quantity and quality of time in His presence. Over the course of 60 days, you'll allow the Spirit more ability to work in you so that you not only do what is good and right, but you do it NATURALLY and INSTICTIVELY. D60 will not only mean better behavior — it will mean deep spiritual transformation.

Would you like to end spiritual failure? Do you want to be spiritually strong?

If you have the heart for it, you can be more than a better person; you can be a different one…. in just sixty-days!

# THE 60 DAYS OF DISCIPLESHIP

# WEEK 1: BASE CAMP

> The first section of <u>D60</u> develops **consistency through the practice of daily habits.**

"Go make disciples…." *Matthew 28:19*

At this point, we are switching from Rocky Balboa to a different rocky analogy—mountain climbing. Step out of the boxing ring and prepare to summit Mt. Everest. This week you are at Base Camp. Here you will gather gear, get instructions, and plot your course as you prepare for your eight-week adventure. In sixty days you'll return to Base Camp inspired, transformed, and spiritually strengthened.

Jesus will be your guide. Through each section of the climb you will follow in His steps listening to him, learning from him, and summiting spiritual heights where only he can lead you. Like any mountain guide, Jesus expects his followers to step where he steps. Make a personal commitment to follow his teachings. They are necessary equipment for navigating the hills and valleys of the mountain. Life's grand vistas are all precluded by slippery slopes and rocky times. Jesus' insights and revelations will safeguard you on the way to the top.

CONSISTENCY—an unwavering and repeated commitment to an idea or direction—is an essential trait of anyone who would follow Jesus. If you consider yourself a disciple of Jesus, live out your commitment to unwavering and repeated obedience. Your first action is simple, but enormously important: say aloud to yourself (and preferably someone else), "I commit to consistently follow the guidance of God for the next sixty days."

Spiritual strongmen don't rise from the baptismal grave -- spiritual babies do. Spiritual strongmen are developed. Faithfully practiced, the exercises and information in this sixty-day program will produce spiritual strength and stamina. The cold fact is that spiritual weaklings will fail to complete this journey. Make up your mind not to be among them. The higher elevations of the climb are very demanding, and unfit climbers won't survive, so pledge now to turn your spiritual flab into spiritual muscle and commit to completing the entire journey.

State your pledge aloud, "I commit to follow the guidance of God for the next sixty days." Somewhere find and note the date that is 60 days from this one, and then proceed to habit #1--"First-Light Prayer."

• • • • • • • • • • • • • • • • • • • • • • • • • • • • • • • • • • • • • • • • • • • • • •

# HABIT #1: FIRST-LIGHT PRAYER

" LORD, Here I am. Help me. "

This simple prayer is how you will begin every morning of this journey. As soon as the first light of day meets your eyes, even before your feet touch the floor, pray,

"Lord, Here I am. Help me."

First-Light Prayer is an amazingly transformational act. It is powerful. As Moses was transformed by God's glory on Mount Sinai, you will begin your days by placing yourself in the presence of God. **First-Light prayer is perhaps the most important habit in <u>D60</u>**. Establishing this simple habit positions you for consistency in more challenging disciplines, but fail to consistently offer a 5-second rote prayer and face likely failure in the more challenging disciplines ahead.

That's it. Short. Simple. Humble. Potent. Unwavering practice of this first habit begins generating strength for overcoming pornography, drug addiction, pride, anger, spiritual weakness, and more. The world's tallest peaks have been mounted, but never without the proverbial "first step." Taking that first step every day is essential to leaving one's footprint at the peak. Consistently placing your first thought on God is the surest path to putting all of them on Him throughout your life.

Paul instructs the Church in Colossians 3:1-2, "Since, then, you have been raised with Christ, **set your hearts on things above**, where Christ is seated at the right hand of God. **Set your minds on things above**, not on earthly things." He then commands his readers to put to death what belongs to the earthly nature. Paul's instruction is that thoughts, controlled and directed heavenward, will aid in victory over the flesh. This principle is applied in the habit of First-Light Prayer.

The First-Light Prayer may seem easy enough, but it is not. Sure, a few people wake their first morning and instantly pray, "God. Here I am. Help me." Many more won't remember until later in the day. A good number will completely forget. DO NOT be discouraged if you are in one of the later two categories. The first days of any training, physical or spiritual, are always challenging, and forming new habits takes a while. Struggling with this new discipline simply illustrates your spiritual condition and affirms the timeliness of your decision to take action. Mastering the HABIT of First-Light Prayer makes the other habits easier to develop.

If you don't remember to pray right away, or at all, don't give up! Simply say the First-Light Prayer as soon as you realize you forgot to pray. This is the Spirit of God speaking to you. It not a defeat; **it is progress!** Remembering your commitment to this habit, even if a belated thought, is from God. Be encouraged! It is the direct working of God in your life. Don't beat yourself up for not immediately thinking to pray; congratulate yourself on hearing His voice! "Oh no! I forgot to pray!" is a change, and, furthermore, it is evidence that a living and growing relationship with God is underway. God is already at work in you! Recognize it, be thankful, and keep moving.

# HABIT #2: THREE-PART READ

Hebrews 4:12 says, "The Word of God is living and active..." Scripture has a power greater than that of an inspirational song, sermon, or book. Scripture is **God**-breathed. It is different. It is alive!

Corn seeds are ground to make cornmeal. Mix cornmeal, liquid, a few other ingredients and then add heat to make cornbread. That hot cornbread will fill your tummy and supply energy for a day or more. But place corn seeds in the ground, add water, allow to warm in the sun, and you'll harvest ears full of corn seeds. Those corn seeds contain energy, **and** they contain life! The Scriptures are as superior to a good Christian book, a sermon, or a song with Christian lyrics as life-giving seed is to tasty cornbread. Spiritual events and products are no substitute for the Scriptures. The Scriptures are **alive!**

*"The **word of God is living and active.**" --Hebrews 4:12*

*"Now I commit you to God and to the **word of his grace**, which can **build you up***

*and give you an inheritance among all those who are sanctified."* **--Acts 20:32**

*"And we also thank God continually because, when you received the word of God… you accepted it not as a human word, but as it actually is, the **word of God**, which is indeed at **work in you** who believe."* **--1 Thessalonians 2:13**

*"For you have been born again, not of perishable seed, but of imperishable, through the living and enduring word of God."* **--1 Peter 1:23**

If, at first, you balk at the notion that God's Word has metaphysical power, please don't. The idea of God's word being powerful and supernatural is as solid and founded as any truth in Scripture. And don't confuse this description of Scripture with anything "new age." This is not suggesting that the Bible is a fetish with special powers. Far from it! This isn't magic, but it is mystery. Mystery is **God's** power at work behind the scenes; magic is **man's** attempt to manipulate unseen power. God's word is mysterious because it contains His breath, and that breath is a mighty spiritual force. As God Himself is, His word is holy, meaning it is "other."

This is not to denigrate sermons or songs, but rather to elevate the Scriptures to their high position. In <u>D60</u> you will feed on the living Word of God because it contains a spiritual life force that can transform you.

Habit #2 is practiced by many people around the world under many titles, but in <u>D60</u> it is called, the Three-Part Read. It is a very powerful tool for placing your thoughts on Scripture and greatly amplifying the Spirit's prospects for transforming you because it is obedience-based; taking the abstract truths of God's Word through your thinking process and into the tangible world. Beyond looking in the mirror and walking away, the Three-Part Read requires action.

*Do not merely listen to the word, and so deceive yourselves. Do what it says. Anyone who listens to the word but does not do what it says is like a man who looks at his face in a mirror and, after looking at himself, goes away and immediately forgets what he looks like, but the man who looks intently into the perfect law that gives freedom, and continues to do this, not forgetting what he has heard, but doing it – he will be blessed in what he does.* **--James 1:22-25**

There are 5 quick steps to the Three-Part Read that should take no more than 20 minutes to complete.

Follow these instructions:

1.  On a sheet of paper, with the widest part running left to right, draw two lines from top to bottom so the paper is divided into three sections.

2.  Label the columns from left to right: "Copy," "My Words," & "I Will."

3.  Select a section of Scripture you'd like to read, (No more than 10 verses) and write a word-for-word copy of your passage in the column labeled "Copy."

4.  Next, write the passage in your own words under the column "My Words." Use language a 12 year old could understand.

5.  In the column labeled "I Will" write what you believe God would have you do with the truth(s) God has shown you in this Scripture. Make your "I will" statement(s) measurable. Instead of writing, "I will pray more," write more specifically, "I will spend ten minutes in prayer today."

As another example, today my Three-Part Read was in Matthew 5:2-12. It is the Beatitudes. My "I Will Statement" was, "I will memorize these verses and repeat them to someone before I sleep tonight." That is measurable. It is also what I thought I should do with the verses.
One more example may be helpful using Daniel 9:4-5.

*"I prayed to the LORD my God and confessed: 'O Lord, the great and awesome God, who keeps his covenant of love with all who love him and obey his commands, we have sinned and done wrong. We have been wicked and have rebelled; we have turned away from your commands and laws."*

A possible statement of commitment could be, *"I will pray and ask God today to show me where I may have turned away from His commands or laws, and I will repent of what He shows me."*

This is easily measured. Measurability helps gauge your obedience to His promptings through His Word.

| Copy | My Words | I Will |
|------|----------|--------|
|      |          |        |

# HABIT #3: TIMED PRAYER

There is one more habit for this first week. If you are feeling overwhelmed, RELAX! These first three habits *combined* should take no more than 35 minutes of your day.

Habit #3: Timed Prayer may appear to be prayer practice. It isn't. Timed Prayer is the habit of ENTERING GOD'S PRESENCE for a limited period each day. In a later week of <u>D60</u> prayer is discussed more in-depth, but the *habit* of praying is this week's focus. Marathoners don't work on speed until they've established a training routine and increase endurance. Regularly placing yourself before God is strategic in building spiritual strength and stamina.

For this habit you will need a watch, clock, or timer. Each day this week, for 15 minutes (not more and not less) you will place yourself in God's presence in an attempt to communicate with Him. You may find it hard to focus your thoughts, or a struggle to fill the entire 15 minutes without repeating yourself. You may daydream. Interruptions, distractions, and drowsiness are to be expected. Do not allow difficulty in focusing to discourage you. While a clear-minded prayer is your ultimate hope, your objective *at this point* is to BE IN THE PRESENCE of God TRYING to communicate with Him DAILY.

If you fall asleep, or your mind wanders, collect yourself, glance at the clock, and say, " God, sorry. I fell asleep. Lord, I've got a little time left. So, I'll try again." Then remain in God's presence and keep trying to communicate until your 15 minutes is completed. If the 15 minutes has already expired, pray, "Sorry, Lord. I'll try again tomorrow. Help me." That's it. Simple. Do-able. Effective. Transforming. Keep at it. **IT WILL GET EASIER**.

What was just described is probably the experience of most people during their first days of Timed Prayer. But some immediately enjoy a euphoric quarter-hour soaring in the heavenlies. If this is your experience then you MUST handle it properly. When your alarm sounds, you will think, "No way! I can't leave now! This is wonderful!" At this point you must STOP! **Immediately** close saying, "Lord, this is wonderful. You are wonderful, and I want to stay longer, but my time is up and I'll be back tomorrow. Love you...bye." Do NOT continue praying. You may certainly talk again with God later, but your goal in this exercise goes beyond a one-time mountaintop experience with Him. The strength you feel today can easily weaken on a day when the climbing is more difficult or less rewarding. You need to develop discipline in order to keep yourself in God's presence every day for the rest of your life. When you develop that consistency and discipline, you'll be on your way to true heights of joy with God. Again, in a later leg of the <u>D60</u>

journey you will develop your prayer life. Keep reminding yourself that <u>D60</u> is about HABITS. This week's goal is to master the discipline of *consistently* ENTERING HIS PRESENCE.

My personal routine is to pray in the morning after a cup of coffee, but before breakfast. Entering His presence at the onset of a day better prepares me for the challenges and opportunities in it. You determine a 15-minute time period that works best for you (lunch, break-time, the drive to work/class, etc.), and present yourself before Him daily. BE THERE. TRYING. CONSISTENTLY.

That's it! Those are the 3 habits to be mastered at Base Camp. Keep track of your progress by using the <u>D60</u> Accountability Chart. The <u>D60</u> Accountability Chart is like an honest friend pointing out your strengths and weaknesses. The self-discipline of completing your chart is itself a spiritual muscle-building exercise. Empty boxes highlight missed opportunities for transformation. You can't get a tan by simply wishing for it. You will not climb the mountain's peak if you don't take the first steps at the foot of it. You don't want any empty boxes. Complete your charts.

## Spiritual Bodybuilding

Almost all physical training includes changes in diet. Most diet plans include mineral, protein, or vitamin supplements. Athletes in training also eliminate unhealthy foods from their menu. In <u>D60</u> there are new habits you'll add, and some unhealthy ones you'll discard.

Romans 6 reads, "*...no longer using the instruments of your body for unrighteousness, but for righteousness.*" Paul is referring to eyes, ears, hands, feet, and mouths. Your body can affect your spirit. **Caring for "the instruments of your body" will help you practice the habits of week #1!**

Three Key Base Camp Practices are **STRONGLY** recommended.

Use your body to help your spirit. 

## Three Key Base Camp Practices:

1. **Control your Rest:** Be in bed no later than midnight and be out of bed no later than 9 a.m. After a few days adjusting, you'll be more alert and able to focus your thoughts. You need all the help you can get to gain control of your mind, and being physically rested is essential in that process.

There are circumstances such as sick children, emergencies, third-shift jobs etc. that will prohibit the suggested sleep schedule. Some exceptions are understandable, but when they happen it is important to adjust not abdicate! At all cost, continue to practice the habits *as best you can* until your schedule can be controlled again. Don't stop; shift.

If you normally go late into the night watching TV, reading, gaming, texting, or talking you must change. Those who cannot pull themselves awake before 9 a.m. must change too. As physical fitness necessitates getting off the couch, spiritual fitness also requires action. Sloppy sleep patterns are spiritually harmful and MUST be exchanged for discipline. Indiscipline produces spiritual couch potatoes, not strong Believers.

Making changes can be uncomfortable. If you aren't able to fall asleep your first few nights, try telling God. "Well, God, here I am. I can't sleep. What do you want to talk about?" This isn't a time wasting exercise. If you will truly talk with Him, it is likely that He'll send you a thought. Continue your conversation with Him about this thought until you fall asleep. Enjoy these conversations. After a few late-night talks you will begin to relax and feel sleepy by or before midnight. You'll also discover that you wake earlier and focus better.

No matter how late you fall asleep, get out of bed by 9 a.m. *--even if you didn't fall asleep until 6 a.m.!!* This is part of adjusting. It is uncomfortable, but it is progress. Natural fatigue will soon cause you to retire earlier and wake more refreshed. Once you have adjusted, you'll feel better and be more mentally alert throughout the day.

 "I'm a night-owl" is NOT an excuse. Many people believe that they are created with a late-night bent. This is, of course, not true. They have simply trained themselves to be most alert in the evening and, therefore, sluggish early in the morning. They've developed into night-owls over the years but can become morning-doves in no time. Stay with the plan. It works. No excuses.

2. **Control your Appetite:**

- Don't consume stimulating drinks or supplements after 7 p.m. Stimulants work against your system's ability to relax and sleep.  NO CAFFEINE after 7 p.m.!!  (If you are over 40 the rule becomes NO CAFFEINE after 5 p.m.!!)

- Reduce sugar intake. This is not a total omission of sugar in your diet, but limiting it. Back off. Walk away from the second piece of cake. Take one sugar in your coffee instead of two.

- Drink more water.  An extra glass of water at each meal will deliver energy as toxins are flushed from your system. More importantly, your mind will develop greater focus.

3. **Control your Body:** To aid in restful sleep…take a walk every day. Take 15 minutes over lunch, or 30 minutes at home after class or work.  I walk two miles in the mornings along the road near my house.  Don't buy running shorts, cross-trainer shoes, or the How to Run a Marathon manual! Just go for a stroll. Burn some extra energy.  You don't even need to sweat; just move a little more to help your body rest at night. Better sleep refreshes the mind and improves concentration, and your body will thank you.

Taking control of your body in these three key ways are first-steps in using 'the instruments of your body' to maximize spiritual strength. They work.  Do them.

# WEEK 1: <u>D60</u> ACCOUNTABILITY CHART

## BASE CAMP: DAYS 1 - 7

"Put your mind on things above where Christ is seated."

Name: _____ | Dates: __/__/__ to __/__/__

## THE HABITS FOR WEEK 1 OF <u>D60</u>

- I was in bed by midnight
- I was up by 9 am
- I had no stimulants past 7 pm

- I prayed the Prayer of First-Light
- I prayed 15 minutes
- I completed the 3 part Readings

Check the boxes you completed

|  | Mon | Tues | Wed | Thurs | Fri | Sat | Sun |
|---|---|---|---|---|---|---|---|
| Bed by midnight |  |  |  |  |  |  |  |
| Up by 9am |  |  |  |  |  |  |  |
| No stimulants past 7pm |  |  |  |  |  |  |  |
| First-light prayer |  |  |  |  |  |  |  |
| Prayed 15 minutes |  |  |  |  |  |  |  |
| 3 part readings |  |  |  |  |  |  |  |

# PERSONAL NOTES

# WEEK 2: THE APPROACH

Congratulations on returning for Week 2: The Approach!

Be on your guard of these habits becoming routine, ritualistic, or just another form of empty religious legalism. Your heart must remain engaged. <u>D60</u> is neither a rabbit's foot nor a potion. Mystery not manipulation is at work in these exercises. Remain humble before God. A tan, not the tanning process is your goal. Transformation in the inner man is your aim; regular practice of the disciplines is your means.

> Disciples grow spiritually through the habitual practice of spiritual habits.

Imagine yourself on the bank of a wide river. If you can swim, how far do you imagine you could swim in a strong current? Three

miles? Five miles? Most of us aren't strong swimmers, but probably most of us can tread water or float. Imagine yourself floating or treading water in the mighty Mississippi River. Caught in that flow, allowing it to carry you, you might easily travel 3-4-5 or more miles in a short time. Entering the flow of God's Spirit will carry you farther spiritually than you can carry yourself. You step into a strong current when you practice these daily habits, and are transported through spiritually deep waters by placing yourself in the flow of God's mind and Spirit.

Spiritual growth results as much from the habit of practice as from the practice of the habits. Consistently presenting yourself before God and putting your mind on Him spiritually strengthens you.

Consistency begins as a decision in favor of some idea or direction, but more is required. A decision to follow Christ must be coupled with "regular actions" to fully mature. Habits are the beach where the Son makes us new. They are the workout room where the heavy lifting of spiritual change takes place. Daily presentation of one self before God is where the branch joins the Vine.

> " Prayer is friendship not business. "

● ● ● ● ● ● ● ● ● ● ● ● ● ● ● ● ● ● ● ● ● ● ● ● ● ● ● ● ● ● ● ● ● ● ● ● ● ● ● ● ● ● ● ● ● ● ● ● ● ● ● ● ●

# HABIT #4: CONFESSION & LISTENING

Having established the basic habits in week 1, you're now ready to climb. In mountaineering terms, the start of a technical climb is called "the approach." Although this is generally a walk, or at most, a scramble, it is occasionally as hazardous as the climb itself. Everything can be lost on the approach.

**Your Approach will focus on two objectives:**

First, drilling your new habits into your schedule. Consistency has been mentioned earlier, but it is so critical that it is impossible to overemphasize its importance. Consistency will be a continued emphasis in week two.

Second, the habits of confession and listening, like the up and the down of a complete push-up, will be learned and practiced in order to develop your budding spiritual muscles this week.

These two new habits are actually forms of prayer. Most praying these days is essentially shopping or wish making. Spiritual shoppers present themselves at the god-store with a list of what they need or want, and wait to see how much is delivered. This is a misunderstanding of prayer. Prayer is relational not contractual; meaning it is more like friendship than business, and best likened to a walk in the park, a drive in the country, or a cup of coffee with God. Certainly, requests are permitted and needs may be expressed, but the emphasis of prayer time in His presence should always be on fellowship and companionship—being *together*.

You know how to talk to God, right? You just start talking, which is easy and natural, and true as far as it goes, but conversation is two-way. When does God talk during prayer, and how do we hear? Prayer is not a monologue. Relationships are two sided, and if God isn't talking, then how is a meaningful relationship being experienced? This week you listen for God and experience relationship.

If you have never heard Him before, the problem hasn't been with God. He doesn't keep silent. John 10:27 says, "My sheep listen to my voice; I know them, and they follow me." The problem's that either you haven't stopped to listen, or that you are spiritually hard of hearing.

Newborns can't see well for the first several weeks; their eyes need development. Spiritual newborns can't hear very well; they need to develop, and it is done through the practice of listening. However, if you're expecting a thunderclap, or straining for a still small voice, you will be disappointed. Don't expect anything audible. Rather, listen for His voice in your thoughts.

You may react to this notion at first, but it really isn't odd or unusual. Many Christians have said something like, "The Devil made me do that," "Something was telling me to do XYZ," or "I had a feeling about that." We often receive ideas from an intangible source. Is it beyond the realm of possibility, even predictability, that God may "speak" a wise or cautionary word to us on occasion? Would it be out of character for him to counsel us with His thoughts?

This week you will learn if God has any thoughts for you. How? You will ask Him. As you wake each morning, you will pray the short First-Light Prayer from week 1 and add a question. Your First-Light Prayer this week will be:

"LORD, Here I am. Help me.
LORD, What needs to change in me?"

When you've prayed, pause. Listen. Pay attention. What thought(s) do you have? If there is no word, then continue your day as usual. If you are encouraged or affirmed, humbly give thanks. If, however, there is a word of counsel for you, embrace it. At some point, as you practice the habits of listening and confessing, God will reveal your failings and weaknesses. When He does, admit them, renounce them, and ask Him to change them. In Scripture this is called "godly sorrow."

*"Godly sorrow brings repentance that leads to salvation and leaves no regret, but worldly sorrow leads to death."* **--2 Corinthians 7:10**

Godly sorrow is not like worldly sorrow. Worldly sorrow feels bad for getting caught, and possibly even for the harm it causes, **but it does not intend to change**. Godly sorrow leads to repentance - repentance is a change of mind toward something, and it leads to a living and healthy relationship with God. Worldly sorrow feels bad and sometimes produces regret, but does not lead to change. Worldly sorrow continues in a direction away from God and thus to spiritual death.  It keeps acting and thinking as it always has.

> Worldly sorrow produces regret...
> **Godly sorrow produces repentance.**

The aim of these new habits is to position you into the flow of the Spirit so He may transform you through your relationship.

*"Now the Lord is the Spirit, and where the Spirit of the Lord is, there is freedom. And we all, who with unveiled faces contemplate the Lord's glory, are being transformed into his image with ever increasing glory, which comes from the Lord, who is the Spirit."* **--2 Corinthians 3:17-18**

Please, don't expect an audible voice, and don't be disappointed if you have no thoughts at all. This is not a rabbit's foot! Don't expect God to obey you. Simply place yourself in a position to better hear IF He has something to say. When He does, you will know it. Trust me. Trust Him.

# HABIT #5: NIGHT JOURNAL

Another habit you'll add this week is "Night Journaling". This is NOT keeping a diary. They are not the same.  A diary is writing down what you did in the day; a journal is writing down what GOD did in the day. A journal is an additional way you will put your mind on God, and increase your time in His presence.  As you have developed the habit of opening each day with your mind on God using the Prayer of First-Light, now close your days with thoughts of Him through the practice of Night Journaling.

## " HINT: Keep your journal beside your bed. "

An expensive journal is not necessary. A spiral notebook is sufficient. Loose sheets of paper work too. I, however, discourage the use of your computer. Handwriting, being slower for most of us, forces our minds to hold the thoughts a little longer. Handwriting is also, in some respects, more personal, even more intimate. Slow down. Linger in His presence. Permit these brief times to be as personal as possible. So, write, don't type, your journal entries.

Your journal entry may be only 2-3 sentences. That is enough. You aren't detailing what you did in your day, just recording what **God** did in your day. Note thoughts or events you believe may have been God working in your life. If there was nothing, then write that as well. Write something like, "Today I followed the D60 routine, and I'm journaling tonight, but I can't see any specific way in which I saw God at work in my life today. I will watch for Him again tomorrow."

It is less important, now, that you recognize any specific activity of God in your life, than that you **LOOK for his activity**. Keep it up. There are great things ahead.

This habit, along with the others, helps put your mind on Him more than is typical. Practicing them, you are floating along in the flow of God's presence. As you abide in the Vine more and more, change will occur. Give Him time.

**HINT**: It is really important to have your journal and a pen beside your bed. You are more likely to reach over and grab a conveniently placed journal than to flip on the lights and search for it in another room. Go now and place it by your bed in preparation for tonight's entry.

# HABIT #6: ANCHORING YOUR MIND

Climbers need anchors. Anchors are metal pins or spikes that are driven into rock. They connect climbers to the mountain in case of a slip or misstep. Anchors are lifesavers. You must anchor yourself to the Rock of Ages. Your anchors are the truths of the Scriptures. For the next few weeks you will be memorizing God's Word. Memorization drills the Scriptures deeply and securely into your center, and gives the Spirit a means of catching you in case of a slip or misstep.

I will suggest a list of verses each week that agree with the habits and teaching for that week. You will find these in your weekly Accountability Charts. My suggestion is that you work on memorizing one of these verses each day. Whether you are able to memorize it perfectly or not is less important than that you are *working at memorizing* it throughout the day. As always, the aim is to put your mind on Him more than ever, allowing Him to change you.

If memorization isn't your thing, I can relate. It sounds difficult and time consuming, but it doesn't need to be. Memorization can be done while doing other things like driving, brushing your teeth, taking a coffee break. You may need to be creative. Try writing your verses on sticky notes and placing them on your mirror, fridge, or computer screen. Make them the home screen on your phone or wallpaper on your computer. If you exercise, repeat them aloud when on your walk, run, or ride. Turn them into songs. Find a way to make it fun and doable.

Anchoring is essential to your spiritual life. When you slip, they'll save you from falling.

● ● ● ● ● ● ● ● ● ● ● ● ● ● ● ● ● ● ● ● ● ● ● ● ● ● ● ● ● ● ● ● ● ● ● ● ● ● ● ● ● ● ● ● ● ● ● ● ● ●

## Gearing Up

Base Camp preparations of week 1 included the "First-Light Prayer," "Timed

Prayer," and "The Three-Part Read". IF you have mastered the DAILY PRACTICE of those habits (in other words, if you are practicing them DAILY), you are ready to move ahead.

This week, add five minutes to your "Timed Prayer". During your 20 (TWENTY) minutes of prayer, you will pray the "I Will" statement(s) of that day's "Three-Part Read." In the evening, you will also make some notes about God's dealings with you in regard to your "I Will" statement. I hope you are beginning to see how the habits learned at Base Camp are essential for your journey in spiritual strengthening. If you have not yet mastered the DAILY practice of the Base Camp habits, please, **do not proceed.** Return to base and master them first. Once you have a solid week of practicing the habits (without missing a day), you can proceed with this week's activities. This is a rule of thumb that should be followed throughout D60: proceed only when the current week's habits have been mastered.

## Summary

Progress may have seemed slow to this point, but you are actually moving along nicely. The first few weeks are an investment in the formation of consistency. Once you have established the habit of practicing the habits, you'll be equipped to move ahead rapidly. Hang with it and trust the plan.

This week you'll be abiding in Christ by consistently practicing these habits:
* First-Light Prayer
* Listening and Confession
* Three-Part Read
* Timed-Prayer for 20 minutes about your "I will" statements
* Anchoring to God's Word through memorizing this weeks' memory verses
* Journaling thoughts related to your "I will" statement(s).

## Final Word:

This may seem overwhelming, as if it will take too much time. Don't believe that lie! You **can** do ALL of these. They should actually take a **total** of only 45 minutes to 1 hour. (The average American watches 4 hours of TV.) You can do this without burdening your schedule (unless it is your TV viewing schedule.) If you are investing more than 90 minutes a day, you need to reduce your time investment, because you are running risk of burnout. Try keeping the Three-Part Read selection to two or three verses. Make only one or two "I Will" statements. Choose shorter memory verses for Anchoring or choose one new verse every two days instead of daily. Keep Night Journal entries to no more than 10 sentences. The aim is for you to place yourself (your mind/thoughts) before God more and more, but you don't want to hurt yourself as you build up your strength. Athletes can injure a muscle because they try too much too quickly. You too can spiritually hurt yourself and suffer a setback. Pace yourself. Stay within the D60 guidelines.

Track your progress by using the Accountability Chart for Week 2

If you need motivation, recall Jesus' question to Peter,
**"Could you not wait with me one hour?"**

# WEEK 2: <u>D60</u> ACCOUNTABILITY CHART

## THE APPROACH: DAYS 8 - 14

"Can YOU keep watch One hour?"

Name: _____ | Dates: __/__/__ to __/__/__

## THE HABITS FOR WEEK 2 OF <u>D60</u>

- I was in bed by midnight
- I was up by 9 am
- I had no stimulants past 7 pm
- I prayed the Prayer of First-Light adding confession

- I prayed 20 minutes
- I completed the 3 part Readings
- I completed my night journaling
- I anchored my mind in God's word

### Check the boxes you completed

|  | Mon | Tues | Wed | Thurs | Fri | Sat | Sun |
|---|---|---|---|---|---|---|---|
| Bed by midnight |  |  |  |  |  |  |  |
| Up by 9am |  |  |  |  |  |  |  |
| No stimulants past 7pm |  |  |  |  |  |  |  |
| First-light prayer |  |  |  |  |  |  |  |
| Prayed 20 minutes |  |  |  |  |  |  |  |
| 3 part readings |  |  |  |  |  |  |  |
| Journal entry |  |  |  |  |  |  |  |
| Anchored in Word | Col 3:1 | Rom 8:5 | 1 Tim 4:16 | Jn 10:27-28 | 2 Cor 7:10 | 2 Cor 3:17-18 | Ps 1:1-3 |

# PERSONAL NOTES

# WEEK 3: FIRST ASCENT

•••••••••••••••••••••••••••••••••••••••••••••

*A first ascent is when a climber or climbers are the first people to climb a route, whether it is a short sport route, a top-rope route, a big wall, a boulder problem, an ice fall, or a mountain. Climbers who make the first ascent of a route give them their identifying names.*

Welcome to Week 3! Things are about to get moving, and you can expect to realize some "upward" movement in your spirit soon. The most exciting parts are still ahead, and week 3's habits will quickly advance your personal spiritual transformation.

Now, let's look at this week's first habit: Instant Obedience.

## Delay is Deadly

John 10:27-28 teaches that Jesus' sheep listen to his voice. It says that they follow him and He knows them. You've been listening for the voice of Christ in your First-Light Prayers. Now you'll further develop your spiritual muscles by listening for His voice and then **obeying Him instantly**.

# HABIT #7: INSTANT OBEDIENCE

It is essential both to hear the word of God, and to obey it --immediately. Delay is deadly. When obedience is delayed, it allows Satan to steal an opportunity to draw nearer the Lord. This week you will practice obeying Him **instantly**.

In the book of Joshua, chapters 6 and 7, the LORD gives Joshua certain commands. In Joshua 6:16, 7:10 and several other places, the record shows that Joshua carried out those commands. I noticed that he always obeyed immediately. Scripture describes his action saying, "Joshua got up early in the morning." He got right to work, as soon as possible, on God's wishes. It must become your habit too.

Rebecca is another example of one who was quick to attend to the things of God. When the servant of Abraham came to her, she *quickly* lowered her water jar and gave them water. Later on she *ran* to her mother to tell the news of the visitor.

Abraham is another example. He *ran* to get food for his guests in Genesis 18 verse seven.

Jesus said, "I do exactly what I have heard from my father." To be a disciple of Christ is to do exactly what our heavenly father says, and to do it as a matter of urgent priority. It is a godly trait to obey God *quickly*.

King Saul exemplified the opposite behavior in I Samuel 15:22. Samuel asked the King about the battle with the Amalekites. God had instructed Saul to destroy everything involving the Amalekites, but Saul had kept some of the livestock and the Amalekite king alive. When Samuel heard this he flew into a rage! God was furious as well. Samuel rebuked Saul, scolding him, "To *obey* is better than sacrifice, to *heed* is better than the fat of rams." *1 Samuel 15:22*

Saul tried to excuse himself by explaining that he'd spared the best flocks, and the King, in order to offer them as sacrifices to God. On the surface this sounded noble, but it was actually rebellion. To give God the things that we want Him to have, but not the things that He wants, is rebellion - it is rebellion because it is doing what *we* want rather than what *God* wants. Delayed obedience to God is a form of rebellion. Putting your wishes, your timetable, your priorities ahead of His are to place yourself before Him. It is important to obey quickly.

The results of King Saul's decisions were devastating. The King and the Israelites are eventually defeated because of Saul's disobedience, but the ramifications don't end there. A generation later, under Queen Esther, the Jews existence as a race is threatened when Haman, the descendant of the same King Agag --whom Saul was told to execute-- has a decree passed to exterminate them. Hesitation to enact the will of God risks devastating consequences to you, your children, and future generations.

You may wonder, "How can I know when God is talking to me?" That's a great question. Here is my answer: "You will know." You will just know it. This sounds a little mysterious, because it is mysterious. Sure, it is open to subjectivity and misunderstanding, but you are protected from falling into danger. How are you protected? Your anchors protect you. The Word of God will keep you on solid ground and safe. **Every thought must be brought into the light of Scripture**. Any "message" or "call to action" that *you think* you are getting from God MUST agree with the teachings and principles of God's Holy Word. Make sure you are bolted to the Scriptures and you won't fall into traps or away from His blessings.

If you listen, you will hear if He has any work for you. I don't mean you hear a voice from the sky, but I do mean that you will have, through your thoughts, a communication from God. God can work through thoughts. Just as we believe that Satan tempts us with evil thoughts, we can know that God directs our steps with righteous thoughts.

As an example, the thought of a kindness you could do for someone may come to mind. He may ask you to delete some action or attitude from your life. God may guide you not to do something you had intended to do, or He may ask you to be still and wait upon him. I have no idea, but I do know that when His thoughts are known, if you will instantly obey them, He will meet you in that obedience. **His thoughts will always agree with those He has revealed in Scripture**. As you learn to hear his voice and obey, you'll begin a dynamic relationship with him. Discipleship is a relationship. Start listening, follow with obedience, and you will experience this relationship.

Though this habit is spiritual in nature, it is also a very common and natural process. Developing a relationship with another person by merely reading about them, or listening to their voice on CD, or talking without listening to their replies will not work. In truth, such a one-sided association isn't a relationship. A relationship involves both parties. It means two-way communication and activity *together*. This week grow in the LORD by listening to Him and join Him where He calls you.

If it seems there are no thoughts from Him in the beginning, relax. It is okay. This is something God decides. The important thing for you is to be in the river of His grace and fixing your thoughts on things above. Be patient. You are in a safe place when you position yourself to hear His voice. Keep doing the right things, and you will reap life-changing results. Don't try to manipulate God; center on being available to Him.

> God will never ask you to do anything contrary to the ways of Jesus or the text of Scripture.

● ● ● ● ● ● ● ● ● ● ● ● ● ● ● ● ● ● ● ● ● ● ● ● ● ● ● ● ● ● ● ● ● ● ● ● ● ● ● ● ● ● ● ● ● ● ● ● ●

# HABIT #8: PRAYING SCRIPTURE

This week, for the first five-minutes of your Timed Prayer, read or quote your memory verse for the day. Spend those five short minutes talking with God (or asking Him) about that verse. Ask for insight. Ask for Him to make you a living model of the truth(s) of that text. I encourage you to write your prayer each time. (Though it is not required.) Some of you may find 20 minutes a long time to keep focused; writing will improve your focus.

Here is an example of praying through a Scripture using 1 Samuel 15:22:

> **"To obey is better than to sacrifice, and to heed is better than the fat of rams."**
>
> *"God,*
> *Your Word says, 'To obey is better than sacrifice, and to heed is better than the fat of rams.' I believe this is true. I am certain that obeying is better than sacrificing. It is always better to do what You want than to do what I'd want. It's better for me to put my life on the altar than it is to put something else on the altar. It's better for me to donate my whole self than to give a few dollars. It's more loving for me to obey you first, than to do what I want, and later apologize. You know best, and I need to trust and obey you. Help me to give you the best part of me. God, my prayer today is that you help me to obey you-- quickly. Help me to be able to hear your voice. I don't hear very well, but I want to, so please help me."*

For the last 5 minutes of your 20-minute Timed Prayer, pray the "I Will" statements you wrote on last week's "Three Read" assignment, or add current "I Will" statements from this week.

# WEEK 3: <u>D60</u> ACCOUNTABILITY CHART

## FIRST ASCENT: DAYS 15 - 21

> " "My Sheep listen to my voice" "

Name: _____ | Dates: __/__/__ to __/__/__

## THE HABITS FOR WEEK 3 OF <u>D60</u>

- I was in bed by midnight
- I was up by 9 am
- I had no stimulants past 7 pm
- I prayed the Prayer of First-Light adding confession

- I prayed 20 minutes using my memory anchor for the day
- I completed the 3 part readings
- I completed my night journaling
- I anchored my mind in God's word
- I listened and obeyed instantly

### Check the boxes you completed

|  | Mon | Tues | Wed | Thurs | Fri | Sat | Sun |
|---|---|---|---|---|---|---|---|
| Bed by midnight |  |  |  |  |  |  |  |
| Up by 9am |  |  |  |  |  |  |  |
| No stimulants past 7pm |  |  |  |  |  |  |  |
| First-light prayer + confession |  |  |  |  |  |  |  |
| 20 min timed prayer using scripture |  |  |  |  |  |  |  |
| 3 part readings |  |  |  |  |  |  |  |
| Journal entry |  |  |  |  |  |  |  |
| Anchored in Word | Ps 56:3-4 | Josh 24:15 | Ps 84:1-2 | Deut 6:4-7 | Deut 6:8-9 | 1 Cor 2:10-13 | Jn 8:12 |
| Instant Obey |  |  |  |  |  |  |  |

# PERSONAL NOTES

# WEEK 4: AN ALPINE START

A tendency to climb in the morning has led to the term "Alpine Start." An "Alpine Start" is an early start that ranges from starting at 11:00 p.m. of the night before on long routes, to just prior to sunrise for shorter routes or faster parties. An "Alpine Start" must begin in the dark.

We look to Joshua again, as an example of someone who practiced the 'Alpine Start' in his life.

- **Early in the morning** Joshua and all the Israelites set out from Shittim…" *Josh 3:1*

- "So Joshua got up **early the next morning** and the priests took up the ark of the LORD." *Josh 6:12*

- "On the seventh day, they got up at **daybreak** and marched around the city…" *Josh 6:15*

- "**Early the next morning** Joshua had Israel come forward by tribes, and Judah was taken." *Josh 7:16*

- "**Early the next morning** Joshua mustered his men, and he and the leaders of Israel marched…" *Josh 8:10*

- *"**After an all-night** march from Gilgal, Joshua took them by surprise..."*
  *Josh 10:9*

Our discipleship begins before we wake. It starts the night before, as we set our alarm clocks, place our journals beside our beds, ask that the first conscious thought of the next day be one of God. Those who practice the Alpine Start advance most quickly.

Joshua's faith in God strengthened beyond that of the millions of other Jews of his generation, and there is a good reason -- Joshua intensely desired to know God, and he took advantage of opportunities to be near Him.
We have only a few, and brief, references to Joshua the pre-leader of Israel, but from these we glean a great deal. Above all we learn that Joshua spent extraordinary amounts of time near God, holy people, and holy places.

- Exodus 17:9-14 - This is the first appearance of Joshua. It's the first battle in the wilderness and the time when Moses stands with the staff of God in his hand as the battle rages. Joshua is the leader of those on the ground. **He stands under the staff of God** to do his work.

- Exodus 24:13 - Our second encounter with Joshua. He is with Moses on the Mountain of God. *They* **remained on the mountain 40 days**, and were the only ones not involved in the revelry back at camp with Aaron and the idol.

- Exodus 32:17 - Descending with the 2 stone tables in Moses' hands, Joshua alerts, *"It is the sound of war."* His words were more insightful than might have been appreciated for in fact Israel was prostituting with an idol. There was war-- spiritual war! The Enemy had assaulted God's Kingdom. Note how Joshua is already manifesting the traits of his mentor, Moses, by **demonstrating a regard for the** holiness of the people, things, and **concerns of God**.

- Exodus 33:11 - After speaking with God face-to-face, Moses would return to the camp, "but his young aide **Joshua, son of Nun, did not leave the tent"** (Exodus 33:11). Joshua spent extraordinary amounts of time near the things of God.

Joshua's habit of lingering near the people and things of God made him strong in faith and a powerful leader. This week, you will follow Joshua's spiritual habits of Alpine Starts and Lingering Near God.

• • • • • • • • • • • • • • • • • • • • • • • • • • • • • • • • • • • • • • • • • • • • • • •

# HABIT #9: ALPINE STARTS

Joshua's hallmark custom of early starts mirrors God's created order. God made the sun and moon as a celestial metronome to mark the end of a day and the start of the next. He appointed lights to mark time. He ordered life and continues to monitor it. God still keeps this routine. Hebrews 13:6 says, "Jesus Christ is the same yesterday, today, and forever." It follows that His disciples should be like him by ordering their days and nights.

There is a natural tendency to become sloppy in the practice of the habits. The ball is easily dropped as enthusiasm wanes. Perhaps you've become lax in your practice of one or more of the first eight habits. This week is a good time to re-double your efforts. Give thanks to God for the day past and pray at bedtime each evening for His presence the next morning. Continue rising early enough to practice the morning habits.

• • • • • • • • • • • • • • • • • • • • • • • • • • • • • • • • • • • • • • • • • • • • • • •

# HABIT #10: LINGERING NEAR

Joshua is always near the center of God's presence and activity. Place yourself there this week. Spend extra time near people involved in the work of God. It is not needed that you be engaged in their activities. Simply be near enough to observe. You can certainly enter into the activities, if appropriate, but you aren't being asked to do so. Just go, looking for God. Watch Him working through others.

- **Go where God is engaged against the enemy...** ask God to guide you on this. He is with the spiritually lost. God is near the broken hearted, to revive them. He covers the orphan and widow to protect them from the Accuser. Where you see Him countering the work of the enemy, go there-- join in or just observe, but respond with zeal and humility.

- **Be with God's people...** praise, serve, pray, fellowship with at least one gathering of Christians this week.

- **Keep your ears open for the cries of God's people...** Listen for incidents of joy and rejoice with them. Give ear to words of rebellion or unfaithfulness and address them humbly, but boldly and immediately.

- **Linger near God...** When you notice Him at work in a person, a group, a moment, or event stay there longer than normal. There is a subtle transforming that occurs when you do. Linger.

In Scripture, Joshua speaks very little of Moses. His interest was not Moses, but God. This week, make God your major focus and concern. Speak less about Christian bands, artists, preachers, or mentors. Let your speech be more and more about Him.

●●●●●●●●●●●●●●●●●●●●●●●●●●●●●●●●●●●●●●●●●●●●●●●●●●●●●●●

# WEEK 4: D60 ACCOUNTABILITY CHART

## AN ALPINE START: DAYS 22 - 28

"Be imitators of God"

Name: _____ | Dates: __/__/__ to __/__/__

## THE HABITS FOR WEEK 4 OF D60

- I was in bed by midnight
- I was up by 9 am
- I had no stimulants past 7 pm
- I prayed the Prayer of First-Light adding confession
- I prayed 20 minutes using my memory anchor for the day

- I completed the 3 part Readings
- I completed my night journaling
- I anchored my mind in God's word
- I listened and obeyed instantly
- I lingered near God's things/people

### Check the boxes you completed

|  | Mon | Tues | Wed | Thurs | Fri | Sat | Sun |
|---|---|---|---|---|---|---|---|
| Bed by midnight |  |  |  |  |  |  |  |
| Up by 9am |  |  |  |  |  |  |  |
| No stimulants past 7pm |  |  |  |  |  |  |  |
| First-light prayer + confession |  |  |  |  |  |  |  |
| 20 min timed prayer using scripture |  |  |  |  |  |  |  |
| 3 part readings |  |  |  |  |  |  |  |
| Journal entry |  |  |  |  |  |  |  |
| Anchored in Word | Matt 5:3-12 | Mat 5:3-12 | Mat 5:3-12 | Deut 6:8-9 | Deut 6:8-9 | Neh 1:7 | Hos 14:1 |
| Instant Obey |  |  |  |  |  |  |  |
| Lingered near to God |  |  |  |  |  |  |  |

# PERSONAL NOTES

# WEEK 5: FREE CLIMB

●●●●●●●●●●●●●●●●●●●●●●●●●●●●●●●●●●●●●●●●●●●●●●●●●●

*Free-climbing is when a climber ascends a rock face using only his hands and feet, as opposed to aid climbing where he places gear and either grabs it or stands in **aiders** to make upward progress. Free-climbing is perhaps the highest and most aesthetic expression of the climbing game since it requires strength, ingenuity, skill, and experience to be successful on the most difficult routes.*

Jesus free-climbed with God. He did it by getting in a boat, walking into a garden, spending the night on a mountain. Putting aside the temporal activities which satisfied others, enabled them to cope, or made them feel meaningful, Jesus chose to approach God without aides. Even as a child, He sought extra time with God, "Don't you know I had to be about my Father's business?" Jesus illustrates to us the highest form of spiritual progress.

Moses, an early sampling of the coming Messiah, also spent extraordinary time alone with God. On Sinai they visited for 40 days and Moses descended with a glow on his face. Every time afterward, when Moses visited God in the tabernacle, his face would again radiate. Scripture says that, "We too with unveiled

faces reflect the Lord's glory" *2 Corinthians 3:18*.

Would you like for Jesus to shine in your life? Do you desire his glory in you? If so, spend time alone with Him. This week you will add an exercise called "Free Climbing." It is designed to send you out alone with Jesus – just the two of you. It is great! You will love it.

# HABIT #11: FREE-CLIMBING

Everyone is busy, so don't attempt to cram this exercise into an overflowing schedule. Plan ahead. Schedule three get-a-ways with God this week, or over the next two weeks. Each free-climb is listed below and should take about 30 minutes.

1.  **Evenings:** Jesus is our example for evening free-climbing. Your assignment is to cut short a day's activities by 30 minutes. This does not mean add this into a day, but substitute it for something else. Adding another activity will feel exhausting and you'll be unlikely to continue the practice. Instead, substitute this habit in place of a less productive habit like watching TV, spending time on Facebook, or playing video games. Use that half hour to write God a letter, or an email. Write as you would to a friend. Share your hopes, your fears, your questions and concerns. Invite Him to reply.

2.  **Lunch:** Take a lunch break with God on a comfortable park bench, at home at your dining room table, or at a restaurant. Eat alone. Silence your house by turning off music, television, or other electronics. In this quieted environment, enjoy your meal, and talk with God - maybe not aloud if you are in a public place. Begin with thanks for the meal. Be specific, mentioning every item, then move on to talking about enjoying and being thankful for your surroundings, health, the weather, or whatever comes to mind. Chitchat with God. It is okay and

it leads to deeper discussion. If it seems odd, uncomfortable, or weird then recall your first date with your wife or husband. It probably began a little awkward, full of chitchat, and may have included lots of silent pauses. You'll become more comfortable with God in days to come. Keep working at it.

3. **A Walk:** Go on a stroll with God. It may be at a park, or just around your yard or through the house, but walk and talk with Him as you go. Be real. Avoid lists of "give-me's." Talk, ask questions, and listen.

4. **Morning Coffee:** Having your coffee, tea, or breakfast, enjoy a visit with God, like you might with a friend. Don't be "churchy" - be yourself. See where the conversation leads you. You will be surprised and blessed.

NOTE: These four exercises are only suggestions. You may create some others of your own, but none should add any time to your current schedule. They should easily substitute in place of things you are already doing.

# HABIT #12: PRAY THE TABERNACLE

I want you to experience a way to easily increase your time in God's presence. It uses the Tabernacle as a blueprint for your 20-minute Timed Prayer.

The Tabernacle prayer is a simple one I first learned from Pastor David Yonggi Cho of South Korea. Using his example, the details of the Biblical Tabernacle give direction to your prayer. Following the arrangement of the ancient Jewish Tabernacle, your prayer should follow the themes listed in the diagram on the next page.

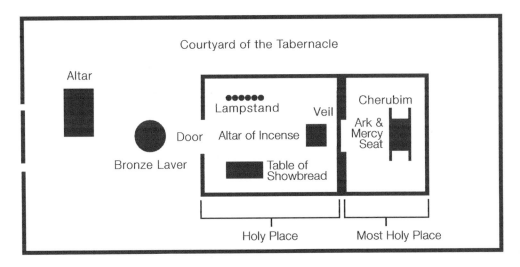

The Jewish Tabernacle

Beginning with the Outer Courtyard and progressing through the Tabernacle, follow the steps of the High Priest into the Holy of Holies. As you approach each element, imagine its spiritual counterpart(s) and allow these to direct your prayer regarding each one.

- **Outer Courtyard:** Pray for those outside of Christ, missionaries far away, or the wandering members of Christ's body.

- **Altar of Sacrifice:** Pray about your own commitment to God. Pray about a fuller surrender to Him. Confess your failures.

- **Bronze Laver:** Ask God to show you (as water in the laver reflected the priest's image) any sins or needs in your life. Pray about whatever He reveals to you.

- **The Entry/Door:** Pause, and consider the rich mercy of God who has allowed you to enter His presence. Give thanks and adoration to Jesus who is the door of your salvation. Consider that He has made you a priest in His service, and talk with (not to) Him about that.

- **The Golden Lamp stand:** Give thanks for the Word, which is a light unto your feet. Pray about the working of the Holy Spirit in your life who appeared to the Apostles as a flaming tongue of fire.

- **The Table of Showbread:** Ask for the daily bread of God in your life. Ask Him to give you direction in this day.

- **The Altar of Incense:** Make your requests and petitions here for your needs and those of others.

- **The Veil:** Give thanks for what Jesus did to take away what separated Jews and Gentiles and has allowed us all to enter the presence of God.

- **The Ark of the Covenant:** This box contained the Ten Commandments, manna, and the rod of Aaron. Pray through the Ten Commandments. Pray and give thanks for God's provisions of daily needs including spiritual ones. Intercede for others as the High Priest did for Israel.

There are more elements in the Tabernacle (e.g. cherubim, gold, incense, mercy seat), which may also be prompts for a variety of prayers. The ones discussed above are a starting place.

This week, pray through the Tabernacle pattern during the 20-minute Timed Prayer.

# WEEK 5: D60 ACCOUNTABILITY CHART

## FREE CLIMB: DAYS 29 - 35

> "Jesus often withdrew to lonely places"
> *Luke 5:16*

Name: _____ | Dates: __/__/__ to __/__/__

## THE HABITS FOR WEEK 5 OF D60

- I was in bed by midnight
- I was up by 9 am
- I had no stimulants past 7 pm
- I prayed the Prayer of First-Light adding confession
- I prayed 20 minutes using the Tabernacle pattern

- I completed the 3 part Readings
- I completed my night journaling
- I anchored my mind in God's word
- I listened and obeyed instantly
- I lingered near God's things/ people
- I had 3 mini-retreats with God

### Check the boxes you completed

|  | Mon | Tues | Wed | Thurs | Fri | Sat | Sun |
|---|---|---|---|---|---|---|---|
| Bed by midnight |  |  |  |  |  |  |  |
| Up by 9am |  |  |  |  |  |  |  |
| No stimulants past 7pm |  |  |  |  |  |  |  |
| First-light prayer + confession |  |  |  |  |  |  |  |
| 20 min prayed Tabernacle |  |  |  |  |  |  |  |
| 3 part readings |  |  |  |  |  |  |  |
| Journal entry |  |  |  |  |  |  |  |
| Anchored in Word | Matt 5:3-12 | Mat 5:3-12 | Mat 5:3-12 | Deut 6:8-9 | Deut 6:8-9 | Neh 1:7 | Hos 14:1 |
| Instant Obey |  |  |  |  |  |  |  |
| Lingered near to God |  |  |  |  |  |  |  |
| 3 mini-retreats |  |  |  |  |  |  |  |

# PERSONAL NOTES

# WEEK 6: FINAL ASCENT

•••••••••••••••••••••••••••••••••••••••••••••••••••••

*Before their final ascent, skilled mountaineers invariably take a series of practice climbs to acclimatize themselves; they go up part way and then return to base camp, over and again, until they are ready for the final push. It is important that each test run have learning value and help shape the best route for the future.*

•••••••••••••••••••••••••••••••••••••••••••••••••••••

## HABIT #13: SEEK A SOUL

Last week you were encouraged to be alone with God because Jesus often retreated to be with God. It was also his practice to be with people.

Jesus spent his days with all sorts of people: elderly and children, sick and healthy, rich and poor, elite and obscure, men and women, Jew and Gentile, saint and sinner. It is likely that you often interact with a variety of people and personalities, but this week you'll be challenged to change your association with them a little. The new habit is called "Seek a Soul." It involves three steps.

**Step 1:** During your First-Light prayer, add a line. Your prayer will now become:

> LORD, Here I am.
> Help me. Help me. Help me.
> What do you want to change in me?
> (This is your new line.) *Lead me to some soul today.*

**Step 2:** Jesus was an expert at recognizing hearts ready for God's grace. Nicodemus, the Samaritan woman, and the Gerasene Demoniac are good examples. Jesus told his followers to lift up their eyes and see the fields ready to harvest. This week be on the look out for souls receptive to salvation. Begin with First-Light Prayer, asking God to lead you to a soul, and proceed with your eyes and ears open! This habit places you near to Jesus by working with (not for) Him, and positions you where God has his greatest concern – the seeking and saving of the lost.

**Step 3:** Prepare nothing but your heart. Leave behind pre-packaged speeches or lessons. Courageously, but humbly, follow Him into these situations—do not try to force them. Remain prepared, and in His perfect way and time the Holy Spirit will aid you! It will be natural. He will give you the words to say, or make your own words effective. Let your concern be to remain with Him. Let Him bear the fruit necessary. Your part is merely to take note of where God may already be active in the life of people you meet, and follow Him in search of those souls.

- **Tears** – Watch for trauma, fear, loss or disappointment affecting anyone around you.

- **Joys** - Watch for births, marriages, promotions, successes, or any event that is producing true happiness.

- **Changes** - Look for those relocating physically, shifting social status, or experiencing relationship changes.

- **Words** - Listen. People will VERY often reveal their hearts through their words. Pay attention to what people are really saying, not just to their words. "I hate my parents," means "My parents and I aren't getting along, and I'm angry about it." Ask God what to do and obey instantly.

This week's habit is another investment in the development of your relationship with Jesus. Exposing yourself to Him through this week's habit will change your life. Keep up the pace. Pray daily. Keep your eyes and ears on alert. Go with Him where He leads. You're getting stronger.

# HABIT #14: TESTIFY

Continue your daily practices, and share with someone what God taught you in Habit #13: Seek a Soul. Avoid sharing with those who may not believe that God works so relationally. Jesus counseled his followers not to cast their pearls before swine, meaning don't give what is valuable to anyone who may not appreciate its value. Use discretion and wisdom; which are not the same as timidity or fear.

## Summary:

Jesus was found among people. This not only included the religious, but very often it included the irreligious. This week you may find that He draws you into those circles. Do not hesitate to join Him. Where He is... you should be also.

# WEEK 6: <u>D60</u> ACCOUNTABILITY CHART

## FINAL ASCENT: DAYS 36 - 42

> "I came to seek and save that which was lost"
> *Luke 9:10*

Name: _____ | Dates: __/__/__ to __/__/__

## THE HABITS FOR WEEK 6 OF <u>D60</u>

- I was in bed by midnight
- I was up by 9 am
- I had no stimulants past 7 pm
- I prayed the Prayer of First-Light asking God to lead me to a Soul
- I prayed 20 minutes using The Tabernacle Pattern

- I completed the 3 part Readings
- I completed my night journaling
- I anchored my mind in God's word
- I listened and obeyed instantly
- I lingered near God's things/people
- I sought for a soul & testified of God's leading me to one.

### Check the boxes you completed

|  | Mon | Tues | Wed | Thurs | Fri | Sat | Sun |
|---|---|---|---|---|---|---|---|
| Bed by midnight |  |  |  |  |  |  |  |
| Up by 9am |  |  |  |  |  |  |  |
| No stimulants past 7pm |  |  |  |  |  |  |  |
| First-light prayer & lead to a Soul |  |  |  |  |  |  |  |
| 20 min prayed Tabernacle |  |  |  |  |  |  |  |
| 3 part readings |  |  |  |  |  |  |  |
| Journal entry |  |  |  |  |  |  |  |
| Anchored in Word | 1 Cor 2:10-13 | 2 Cor 1:3-5 | 2 Cor 1:3-5 | Lk 13:9 | Jn 14:25-27 | Jn 15:26-27 | Zeph 3:12 |
| Instant Obey |  |  |  |  |  |  |  |
| Lingered near to God |  |  |  |  |  |  |  |
| Sought a Soul |  |  |  |  |  |  |  |

# PERSONAL NOTES

# WEEK 7: THE SUMMIT

●●●●●●●●●●●●●●●●●●●●●●●●●●●●●●●●●●●●●●●●●●●●●●●●

From the summit, the whole world looks different. Far, far below rivers appear as threads, yet the clouds hang at arm's length. The task of reaching the top is done; returning to the familiar is now the challenge. But for a few moments climbers must pause to take a breath, look out, gather it all in, and realize where they stand.

Congratulations on reaching "The Summit!" A few weeks ago you got away and alone with God because Jesus often got away from people. The following week, because Jesus was often with people, you joined Him in seeking souls. This week, you will again put your mind on Him, join Him, be with Him, and find Him. This time you will find Him in His creation.

God is often compared to created things. For example: mountains, fire, seas, flowers, light, wind, sound, the sea, lions, and lambs. Creation itself was a teacher whose classes the ancient Psalmists attended.

*The heavens declare the glory of God, the skies proclaim the work of his hands. Day after day they pour fourth speech, night after night they display knowledge. They have no speech, they have no words; no sound is heard from them. Yet, their voice goes out into all the earth, their words to the ends of the world.* **Psalm 19:1-4**

It is possible to see many of God's eternal qualities in your surroundings. They declare the glory of God! Listen!!

●●●●●●●●●●●●●●●●●●●●●●●●●●●●●●●●●●●●●●●●●●●●●●●●●●●●●●●

# HABIT #15: LOOK FOR GOD IN CREATION

This week is exciting. From the summit, you'll pause to look around you to hear what the created things declare about God. In this habit, you are not worshiping the creation, but listening and looking for what the Creator is revealing about Himself through creation.

After your Prayer of First-Light, look out the window. Whatever created thing you see first, let that begin your meditation on God's character by asking, "What does this illustrate about God?" Listen, and thank God for the insight.

For example, after your prayer you may notice the sun rising and consider how consistently the sun rises. God too is consistent. He never changes. He is therefore dependable and faithful. Thank Him for his faithfulness and consistency.

Carry your musing into your 20-minute Timed Prayer. Talk with God about what you saw, and your insight(s). Ask Him for more insights. Perhaps He will bring Scriptures to mind like, "I will never leave you or forsake you." Deuteronomy 31:6. On the other hand, you may be challenged to be more consistent in your relationship with Him. This habit is a tool God can use to teach you about Him, or instruct you about yourself. Give thanks for any insights provided through His creation.

During the day, share your insights with someone else to help them see Him too. Complete the day by writing about all of this in your journal entry.

# HABIT #16: TAKE A HIKE

One day this week take a hike. Stroll in a park, walk down the sidewalk in your neighborhood, or find a place to be alone near a window, but be where you can view God's creation. As you walk (or sit by the window if you can't leave the house), *ask Him* to open your eyes so you can "see" and your ears so you can "hear" what He is revealing about Himself through creation.

Then, *pay attention*. Notice whatever catches your ear or eye. Think about that thing. Watch it for a while. Listen for thoughts God may send about Himself as you ponder His magnificent creation. Talk to Him about it. Tell Him what you *think* He is saying to you. Listen for His response in your thoughts. Allow a conversation to develop, **keeping in mind that nothing you learn will disagree or in any manner be contrary to what He has already plainly revealed about Himself in Scripture.**

The aim here is to be in communion with God, not his creation. The expectation is that He will reveal Himself if you are serious about finding *Him*. Do not practice this habit in pursuit of having an "experience." Simply put your mind on Him in this special way and, by so doing, allow yourself to be transformed as you sit a little longer this day in the presence of God. As always, the heart is the key, never the habit itself.

Lastly, ask yourself, "Where do I now stand with God?" You've come far over the past few weeks. Certainly, you've become aware of changes (deep ones)

God has made in you. Enjoy the view. Take in all you can. Your decent begins next week.

# WEEK 7: <u>D60</u> ACCOUNTABILITY CHART

## THE SUMMIT: DAYS 43 - 49

"God's invisible qualities... being understood from what has been made" *Rom 1:20*

Name: _____ | Dates: __/__/__ to __/__/__

## THE HABITS FOR WEEK 7 OF <u>D60</u>

- I was in bed by midnight
- I was up by 9 am
- I had no stimulants past 7 pm
- I watched for God out my window
- I prayed the Prayer of First-Light reflecting on creation

- I prayed 20 minutes, including what I saw out my window
- I went on a nature walk with God
- I completed the 3 part Readings
- I completed my night journaling
- I anchored my mind in God's word

### Check the boxes you completed

| | Mon | Tues | Wed | Thurs | Fri | Sat | Sun |
|---|---|---|---|---|---|---|---|
| Bed by midnight | | | | | | | |
| Up by 9am | | | | | | | |
| No stimulants past 7pm | | | | | | | |
| Watched for God out window | | | | | | | |
| First-light prayer reflecting on creation | | | | | | | |
| Prayed 20 min + creation outside | | | | | | | |
| Nature Walk w/ God | | | | | | | |
| 3 part readings | | | | | | | |
| Journal entry | | | | | | | |
| Anchored in Word | Ps 19:1-4 | Isa 6:3 | Ps 50:1-3 | Ps 50:3-6 | Isa 4:2-4 | Isa 4:5-6 | Ps 90:1-6 |

# PERSONAL NOTES

# WEEK 8: THE DESCENT

As wonderful as the view is from above, it is time to return to the valley. Beware! The return is not effortless, or without danger. In fact, it can be treacherous, fatiguing, and is often where climbers become careless and plummet to their deaths. You will descend this week from your mountaintop, but you must remain vigilant, for you can easily lose your footing and fall from the heights rather than returning healthy and whole.

Your descent will follow the exact same path of your ascent—only in reverse. This week, each day will retrace the steps found in the previous weeks. This is important because the lessons God has taught you, the messages He has given you, the commitments to which He has led you, and the relationship between you must not be lost. Your efforts this week ensure that the benefits of your first seven weeks are not wasted.

Take each day of this week as follows:

# Day 1

- After your First-Light Prayer, immediately take another look at the item in creation that drew your attention last week. Recall what you learned about God from that item and give thanks.

- Revisit the place or path you went on your hike with God. Talk more with Him about the things He brought to your attention during that hike.

- Review the memory verses from week 7.

- Prepare for bed a few minutes earlier tonight, and re-read your journal entries from week 7. Make a new journal entry after reading them.

# Day 2

- During your 20-minute Timed Prayer, pray again for the person or persons you were led to in week 6.

- Call, write, or visit the person or persons God put on your heart in the week when you asked Him to lead you to some soul. In your communication to them, assure them that God is aware of them, and that you have prayed for them today. Be open to the possibility that God may carry these relationships/conversations farther.

- Review the memory verses from week 6.

- Prepare for bed a few minutes earlier tonight and re-read your journal entries from week 6. Make a new journal entry for today after reading them.

# Day 3

- Pray the Tabernacle prayer during your 20-minute Timed Prayer.

- Spend the day in the presence of Jesus. Talk with him all day long, have lunch alone with Him or have coffee together. Consider it a special occasion before you re-enter the valley ahead.

- Review the memory verses from week 5.

- Prepare for bed a few minutes earlier tonight and re-read your journal entries from week 5. Make a new journal entry for today after reading them.

# Day 4

- During your 20-minute Timed Prayer, talk with God about directing you to some place or person where, or in whom, the Spirit seems to be present.

- Today, attend an event, a meeting, a place, or spend time with a person where or in whom God seems to be present. Do not hurry away, but linger near and be open to the possibility that those who are near the things and places of God find themselves affected by being in His presence.

- Review the memory verses from week 4.

- Prepare for bed a few minutes earlier tonight and re-read your journal entries from week 4. Make a new journal entry for today after reading them.

# Day 5

- Pray through the memory verses from week 3.

- Be attentive to God's voice today. Exercise your spiritual muscles in instant obedience, even in the mundane, all day today.

- Prepare for bed a few minutes earlier tonight and re-read your journal entries from week 3. Make a new journal entry for today after reading them.

# Day 6

- During your 20-minute Timed Prayer, listen more than talk.

- Take a short break with God today and be silent. Listen in case He has something to communicate. Otherwise, simply make yourself available by setting aside a quarter hour and being attentively silent.

- Review the memory verses from week 2.

- Go to bed a few minutes earlier tonight and re-read your journal entries from week 2. Make a new journal entry for today after reading them.

# Day 7

- Today you will really stretch your spiritual muscles by spending 1 hour before the LORD in Timed Prayer.

- Review the memory verses from week 1.

- Prepare for bed a few minutes earlier tonight and re-read your journal entries from week 1. Make a new journal entry for today after reading them.

# WEEK 8: <u>D60</u> ACCOUNTABILITY CHART

## THE DESCENT : DAYS 50 - 56

"Remember the wonders He has done..."
*1Chron 16:12*

Name: _____ | Dates: __/__/__ to __/__/__

## THE HABITS FOR WEEK 8 OF <u>D60</u>

- I was in bed by midnight
- I was up by 9 am
- I had no stimulants past 7 pm
- I prayed the Prayer of First-Light reflecting on creation
- I completed Day 1 assignments

- I completed Day 2 assignments
- I completed Day 3 assignments
- I completed Day 4 assignments
- I completed Day 5 assignments
- I completed Day 6 assignments
- I completed Day 7 assignments

### Check the boxes you completed

|  | Mon | Tues | Wed | Thurs | Fri | Sat | Sun |
|---|---|---|---|---|---|---|---|
| Bed by midnight |  |  |  |  |  |  |  |
| Up by 9am |  |  |  |  |  |  |  |
| No stimulants past 7pm |  |  |  |  |  |  |  |
| First-light prayer |  |  |  |  |  |  |  |
| Morning prayer |  |  |  |  |  |  |  |
| Daily Assignments |  |  |  |  |  |  |  |
| Journal Reading |  |  |  |  |  |  |  |
| Journal entry |  |  |  |  |  |  |  |
| Memory verses |  |  |  |  |  |  |  |

# PERSONAL NOTES

# DAYS 57-60: RECOVERY

●●●●●●●●●●●●●●●●●●●●●●●●●●●●●●●●●●●●●●●●●●●●●●●

After any hard climb, there is a necessary period of recovery. It is important to reassess, to revive, to remember, to relive, and to regroup before a future climb.

## DAY 57: A DAY OF SELF EXAMINATION

Complete the Spiritual Growth Assessment below. Do it. It will yield insights either as an encouragement, or a rebuke, but always for your benefit. To the degree that you practice the habits you will see a corresponding level of growth in your relationship with God. Be honest. Learn where you are weak. Evidence of weakness should not be a discouragement as much as a helpful sign of an area where you are still spiritually flabby. Weaknesses are areas God will strengthen on future climbs.

# D60 - Spiritual Growth Assessment

## Instructions:

Complete each area honestly and as accurately as you are able.

## Consistency:

1. On a scale of 1 to 10, with 10 being "flawless," how consistent were you in implementing the spiritual disciplines...

   - Before D60:                 1   2   3   4   5   6   7   8   9   10
   - My Best Week of D60:     1   2   3   4   5   6   7   8   9   10
   - Currently:                  1   2   3   4   5   6   7   8   9   10

2. I am generally consistent in my daily spiritual habits *less / same / more* than before I started D60. (Circle one.)

3. I feel *more / less / about the same* committed to the spiritual muscle building habits from now on? (Circle one.)

4. I *will / will not* continue to work at these and other spiritual muscle building habits. (Circle one.)

## The Word:

1. On a scale of 1 to 10, with 1 being "never" and 10 being "daily," how often were you reading and applying God's Word...

   - Before D60:                 1   2   3   4   5   6   7   8   9   10
   - My Best Week of D60:     1   2   3   4   5   6   7   8   9   10
   - Currently:                  1   2   3   4   5   6   7   8   9   10

2. I am generally reading God's Word *less/same/more* than before I started D60. (Circle one.)

3. I feel *more / less / about the same* compelled than ever to daily read and

personally apply God's Word from now on? (Circle one.)

4. I *will / will not* continue to daily read and personally apply God's Word. (Circle one.)

## Prayer:

1. On a scale of 1 to 10, with 1 being "never" and 10 being "daily," how often were you praying...

   - Before <u>D60</u>:       1   2   3   4   5   6   7   8   9   10
   - My Best Week of <u>D60</u>:   1   2   3   4   5   6   7   8   9   10
   - Currently:       1   2   3   4   5   6   7   8   9   10

2. I am generally praying *less / same / more* than before I started <u>D60</u>. (Circle one.)

3. I am averaging _____ (hrs / min) a day in prayer. (Make an estimate.)

4. I feel *more / less / about the same* compelled than ever to pray often? (Circle one.)

5. I *will / will not* continue to pray often. (Circle one.)

## Journaling:

1. On a scale of 1 to 10, with 1 being "never" and 10 being "daily," how often were you journaling...

   - Before <u>D60</u>:       1   2   3   4   5   6   7   8   9   10
   - My Best Week of <u>D60</u>:   1   2   3   4   5   6   7   8   9   10
   - Currently:       1   2   3   4   5   6   7   8   9   10

2. I am generally journaling *more / less / about the same* than I was on the first day of <u>D60</u>. (Circle one.)

3. I feel *more / less / about the same* compelled than ever to journal. (Circle one.)

4. I *will / will not* continue to daily journal. (Circle one.)

## Anchoring:

1. On a scale of 1 to 10, with 1 being "never" and 10 being "daily," how often you were anchoring to (memorizing) God's Word...

   - Before <u>D60</u>:            1   2   3   4   5   6   7   8   9   10
   - My Best Week of <u>D60</u>:   1   2   3   4   5   6   7   8   9   10
   - Currently:                    1   2   3   4   5   6   7   8   9   10

2. I am generally memorizing *less / same / more* than before I started <u>D60</u>. (Circle one.)

3. I have memorized _____ more verses than I did 8 weeks ago. (Give a number.)

4. I feel *more / less / about the same* compelled than ever to memorize Scripture? (Circle one.)

5. I *will / will not* continue to memorize God's Word. (Circle one.)

## Listening:

1. On a scale of 1 to 10, with 1 being "never" and 10 being "always," how often were you listening for God...

   - Before <u>D60</u>:            1   2   3   4   5   6   7   8   9   10
   - My Best Week of <u>D60</u>:   1   2   3   4   5   6   7   8   9   10
   - Currently:                    1   2   3   4   5   6   7   8   9   10

2. I am generally listening for God *less / same / more* than before I started <u>D60</u>. (Circle one.)

3. I feel *more / less / about the same* compelled than ever to listen for God. (Circle one.)

4. I *will / will not* continue to listen for God. (Circle one.)

## Instantly Obeying:

1. On a scale of 1 to 10, with 1 being "never" and 10 being "always," how well were you instantly obeyed God...

   - Before D60:            1   2   3   4   5   6   7   8   9   10
   - My Best Week of D60:    1   2   3   4   5   6   7   8   9   10
   - Currently:             1   2   3   4   5   6   7   8   9   10

2. I generally obey instantly *less / same / more* than before I started D60. (Circle one.)

3. I feel *more / less / about the same* compelled than ever to obey God instantly. (Circle one.)

4. I *will / will not* continue obey God instantly. (Circle one.)

## General Assessment:

**T / F**   I am more spiritually fit than I was before D60.

**T / F**   I would have been more spiritually fit if I had done better at the D60 activities.

**T / F**   I have had one or more evidences that the Spirit of God has changed me during these weeks.

List the spiritual fruit born in you during these weeks which has come naturally and seemingly effortlessly—like water from a spring instead of from a well:

_____

_____

_____

_____

_____

_____

_____

_____

My relationship with God is now (Briefly describe): _____

_____

_____

_____

_____

_____

_____

My spiritual muscles are *stronger / weaker / unchanged* since beginning <u>D60</u>. (Circle one.)

My relationship with God is *better / worse / unchanged* as a result of practicing these new habits. (Circle one.)

● ● ● ● ● ● ● ● ● ● ● ● ● ● ● ● ● ● ● ● ● ● ● ● ● ● ● ● ● ● ● ● ● ● ● ● ● ● ● ● ● ● ● ● ● ● ● ● ●

# DAY 58: A DAY OF THANKSGIVING

Talk with God throughout the day, giving thanks to Him, and recognizing Him for the many spiritual blessings, encounters, and special benefits He brought to you during these recent weeks.

Demonstrate your gratitude for these spiritual gifts. You may do this by making a donation to a charity, spending special time with someone who is lonely, or giving a gift to someone totally unsuspecting (or undeserving) who cannot repay you in kind.

## Being Accountable

I demonstrated my gratitude for the many spiritual blessings, encounters, and special benefits God brought to me during these recent weeks. **Y / N** (Circle One.)

# DAY 59: A DAY OF FASTING

Fasting is deep spiritual work. The discomfort of a fast is a physical reminder of what happens when we are away from God. For one meal or more, instead of eating, ask God to make your spiritual pain as great and real as the physical pain of fasting, if ever you should fail to feast on His Word or drink in His life.

## Being Accountable

I fasted for one meal or more this week instead of eating, and I asked God to make my spiritual pain as great and real as the physical pain of fasting, if ever I should fail to feast on His Word or drink in His life. **Y / N** (Circle One.)

# DAY 60: A DAY OF CELEBRATION & FEASTING

Throw a party! Invite people who are not your normal associates or friends to a picnic, a restaurant, or your home. Invite those whom you believe Jesus would invite to a feast.

- **Share the story** of what you've experienced over the last eight weeks, and how God has interacted with you. (Do not preach to them! Do not solicit from them any response. Simply share honestly, humbly, and enthusiastically what the Lord has done for and in you.)

- Tell them -- in honest and non-churchy terms -- your understanding of **how much God loves and cares for *them*.**

## Being Accountable

- I had a party for people who are not my normal associates or friends. I invited those whom I believed Jesus would invite to a party. **Y / N** (Circle One.)

- I shared the story of my experiences and how God has interacted with me over the past 60 days. **Y / N** (Circle One.)

- I told them -- in honest and non-churchy terms -- my understanding of how much God loves and cares for them. **Y / N** (Circle One.)

# A FINAL WORD: THE VALLEY

## A WORD ABOUT THE VALLEY...
## Set low expectations

You have enjoyed special encounters and moments with the Lord these past few weeks, but those who have remained in the valley have not. *Please, do not assume they will appreciate, celebrate, understand, or agree with your experiences.* Even those closest to you may discount your testimony as insignificant or less than what it is. Actually, these responses are predictable and quite normal. Even those who are enthusiastic may only be so on a shallow level. Do not be discouraged. Be gracious to them - after all, you once lived in the valley too. Do not consider yourself better or more spiritual-- only blessed and thankful for having been shown how to grow in these ways.

# A WORD ABOUT DAY 61...
## Climb again!

Pray for those you share with and invite any who seem willing to come with you on next week's ascent - you see, there are always mountains to climb whose peaks are higher still. Your next ascent begins tomorrow. Return to Week 1, Day 1, and launch out on your own mountain climb; selecting the verses you should memorize, the activities you are being led to practice, and the lengths of time which seem best for you and the Lord. Remain in Him and fruit will spring forth in abundance. Be seeing you at the top!

# PERSONAL NOTES

# ABOUT THE AUTHOR

Stephen Meeks and his family served ten years as members of a church planting mission team in Kenya, East Africa among the Kalenjin tribe. The team, working with national evangelists, initiated the planting of over 100 indigenous congregations.

Leaving Africa, Stephen served four years as the Executive Director of Camp Deer Run inc., a Christian camping and retreat facility in Texas. In 1999 he founded GoodSoil Ministries inc. -- a non-profit organization serving missionaries. He is the Executive Director of GoodSoil and is involved in church planting in rural Appalachia.

Stephen, his wife Donna, and their five children have enjoyed simple living on their small farm on the Cumberland Plateau in East Tennessee for the past 18 years where he and his family built their log home.

Stephen's favorite time of the day is morning, when he enjoys a cup of coffee before his regular two-mile walk-n-talk with God that has become a special time they both anticipate.

His other writings include a children's book How to Get a Monkey out of Bed; Voyage of the Euangelia-- an introduction to the fundamental principles and practices of missions; and Beyond the Rituals - thoughts about faith, hope and love drawn from true stories during his decade in Africa.

# SOURCES

Acknowledgements - Quote taken from The 17 Indisputable Laws of Teamwork by John C. Maxwell; Thomas Nelson Publishers, 2001.

Week 3 – Definition of 'first ascent' taken from
http://climbing.about.com/od/dictionaryofclimbing/a/FirstAscentDef.htm.

Week 5 – Definition of 'free climb' taken from
http://climbing.about.com/od/dictionaryofclimbing/a/FreeClimbingDef.htm.

Week 6 - Final Ascent quote taken from Climbing the Mid-Career Mountain by Douglas B. Richardson, Certified Master Coach.

All Scripture quotes are taken from the New International Version of the Bible.

Made in the USA
Lexington, KY
08 November 2014